PUBLIC LIBRARY DISTRICT OF COLUMBIA

D1397072

SEP 0 6 2003

PUBLIC LIBRARY DISTRICT OF COLUMBIA

Fossils

Trudi Strain Trueit

04708-6301
Franklin Watts
A Division of Scholastic Inc.
New York • Toronto • London • Auckland • Sydney
Mexico City • New Delhi • Hong Kong
Danbury, Connecticut

For Nikki, editor extraordinaire,
whose heart for children shines through every page.

Note to readers: Definitions for words in **bold** can be found in the Glossary at the back of this book.

Photographs © 2003: Australian Museum/Nature Focus: 15; AP/Wide World Photos: 6, 7 (Diego Giudice), 4 (Mariano Izquierdo/La Nacion); Corbis Images: 48 (Layne Kennedy), 18 (Michael T. Sedam), 21, 43 right, 43 left; NASA: 25; National Geographic Image Collection/O. Louis Mazzatenta: 38; Peter Arnold Inc.: 45 (Richard Weiss), 37 top (Norbert Wu); Photo Researchers, NY: 35 top, 36 (James L. Amos), 30 (Biophoto Associates), 31 (E.R. Degginger), 3 bottom, 17 (Vaughan Fleming/SPL), 8, 9, 12, 35 bottom (Francois Gohier), 40 (Mehau Kulyk/SPL), 10, 11 (Francis Latreille/Nova Productions), 13 (Andrew J. Martinez), 16 (Newman & Flowers), 37 bottom (Jeff Rotman), 32 top (Mark A. Schneider), cover, 26, 27, 28, 29, 32 bottom (Sinclair Stammers/SPL), 33 top (Kaj R. Svensson/SPL); PhotoEdit/David Young-Wolff: 46; Visuals Unlimited/Ken Lucas: 3 top, 33 bottom, 41.

The photograph on the cover shows a trilobite fossil. Trilobites are an extinct group of marine invertebrates with a hard, segmented shell that is divided into three sections. The photograph opposite the title page shows the excavation site of paleontologist Phil Curie along the Red Deer River.

Library of Congress Cataloging-in-Publication Data

Trueit, Trudi.
    Fossils / Trudi Strain Trueit
        p. cm. – (Watts Library)
    Summary: Presents information on fossils, including how different types are formed, how they have been used to date periods in Earth's history, and major areas of the world where fossil hunting is going on today.
    Includes bibliographical references and index.
    ISBN 0-531-12196-8 (lib. bdg.)   0-531- 16242-7 (pbk.)
    1. Fossils—Juvenile literature. [1. Fossils.] I. Title. II. Series.
QE714.5 .T75 2003
560—dc21   2001008285

©2003 Franklin Watts, a Division of Scholastic Inc.
All rights reserved. Published simultaneously in Canada.
Printed in the United States of America.
1 2 3 4 5 6 7 8 9 10 R 12 11 10 09 08 07 06 05 04 03

Contents

Exposed spine of a dinosaur found in Patagonia, Argentina

Chapter One

Yesterday's World

Gusty winds sweep off the eastern slopes of the Andes Mountains over the vast, silent plains. Not much grows here. Few people live here. The winds are too cold and the ground, too dry. These are the **badlands** of Patagonia, Argentina. Stretching 300,000 square miles (770,000 square kilometers) from the Colorado River to the tip of South America, the largest desert in the Americas is a dusty, barren landscape. Patagonia wasn't always this way, though. Millions of years

Fossil Fever

Besides Argentina, other hot spots for dinosaur fossils include Chad and Niger in Africa, Mongolia, China, and the western United States. A major fossil discovery is reported from one of these places about once a week.

ago, there were lush forests, thick underbrush, and plentiful water here. Patagonia was also home to some of the largest **dinosaurs** in the world.

Today, scientists from around the globe flock to the dinosaur graveyards in Patagonia, hoping to unearth a new link to the past. In the mid-1990s, a team of **paleontologists**—scientists who study **fossils**—made a major discovery. They uncovered a **sauropod** unlike any on record. These plant-eating giants of the dinosaur world had small heads, long necks and tails, and huge bodies supported by elephantlike legs. The paleontologists decided to name their find *Argentinosaurus*. At 125 feet (38 meters) in length and weighing more than 50 tons, *Argentinosaurus* was probably the largest sauropod ever to roam Earth.

Egg-citing Events

Among the two hundred known dinosaur egg sites around the world are Egg Mountain in Montana and the Nemegt Valley in Mongolia. China's Xixia Basin holds the record for the largest dinosaur eggs, measuring up to 18 inches (45 centimeters) in length.

In 1997, a group of American and Argentine paleontologists on a dig in Patagonia stumbled upon a dinosaur nesting ground. The site yielded tens of thousands of softball-sized eggs, many of which enclosed the first sauropod embryos ever found. Inside some of the eggs, scientists made another rare

Paleontologist Luis Chiappe uses his pocketknife to inspect a fossilized group of dinosaur eggs.

These fossilized dinosaur eggs were found in the Xixia Basin in China.

find—fossilized dinosaur skin. Analysis of the bumpy skin identified the embryos as titanosaurs, a type of sauropod with bony, armor-plated skin nodules.

The fossils that are dusted off in Patagonia give paleontologists one more piece of the massive puzzle that is **prehistoric** life. Fossils help us understand what Earth was like millions of

years ago and what kinds of plants and animals inhabited it. They can also reveal the relationships between life then and now. For all fossils have already told us about yesterday's world, however, scientists say we have barely scratched the surface of what is waiting to be discovered. We live on a planet that is continually changing. More than ten million different life forms are alive today. But that is a small number compared to the trillions of organisms that have come and gone since life began on Earth more than 3.5 million years ago. More than 70 percent of all species of land animals and 85 percent of all sea creatures that ever existed on Earth are **extinct**, or no longer alive. Fossils are vital clues left behind from a world we could once only imagine and are now just beginning to understand.

Explorer Bernard Buigues views the tusks of what is believed to be a 23,000-year-old woolly mammoth whose body is preserved in the ice.

Chapter Two

Fossil Birth

Fossils are found on every continent on Earth, from snow-tipped mountain peaks to the sandy edges of an outgoing tide. A fossil is the preserved evidence that an organism once lived on Earth. The word *fossil* means "dug up," but there is far more to fossils than that.

There are three main types of fossil: **body fossils**, **trace fossils**, and **coprolites**. A body fossil may be a mammoth frozen in ice or a mosquito trapped in **amber** (tree resin). It may be the tooth of an extinct reptile or preserved seeds too small to be seen without a microscope. Even the signs of life that animals leave behind—such as their footprints, tail tracks, bite marks, tunnels, nests, and dung—are fossils. These signs are called trace fossils. Scientists rely on trace fossils for insight into the lifestyles of ancient animals. Fossilized footprints and tail tracks can reveal how much an animal weighed, how it moved, and whether or not it lived in a herd. Remains of nesting sites offer hints as to how an animal gave birth and raised its young. Fossilized dung, or droppings, are called coprolites. Coprolites show what food the animal ate and the type of **climate** it lived in.

For an organism to fossilize, it must be buried quickly after it dies. Otherwise it will rot in the open air, be carried off by other animals, or be broken down by chemicals in the soil. Fossils of the imprints of soft tissue parts, such as muscles,

These dinosaur tracks, known as trace fossils, were found in an area now called Dinosaur Ridge near Denver, Colorado.

You can clearly see the fossils in this piece of limestone.

organs, or eggs, are rare discoveries because soft tissues are often eaten by other animals or decay too quickly to be preserved. Hard parts such as bones, teeth, shells, or wood are usually all that is left behind to fossilize. Even then, only about 1 to 2 percent of all life forms will ever become fossils.

Fossils are found only in **sedimentary rock**, such as sandstone, limestone, and shale. This type of rock is made up of sediments, which are particles of older rocks that have been broken apart and **eroded**, or worn down by wind, water, and other forces. These sediments—pieces of sand, gravel, clay, mud, and shells—usually end up at the bottom of lakes, rivers, and oceans. As they settle, sediments bury the remains of plants and animals. Over a long period of time, the increasing weight of the layers compacts and cements the sediments, turning them into rock. Gradually, forces in Earth push the sedimentary rock up toward the surface of the water where it may be exposed. Sandstone is made from grains of sand that have cemented together. Limestone comes from the shells of some animals. Shale is formed from mud and clay.

Preserving the Past

Fossils are preserved through **petrification**, **carbonization**, **freezing**, or being caught in organic traps such as amber. One of the most common types of fossilization is petrification,

Fuel for Thought

Heat and pressure from layers of sediment may turn decaying life forms into coal, oil, and natural gas. These are called **fossil fuels**. Coal comes from the swamplands of ancient forests. Oil and natural gas are made from the bodies of microscopic aquatic organisms. It took hundreds of millions of years to create the fossil fuels that humans rely on today to power cars and heat homes. Scientists say that human beings are using the world's supply of fossil fuels at a much faster rate than nature can replenish it.

which is the partial or complete changing of an organism into rock. There are several ways an organism may be petrified, or "turned to stone." In **permineralization**, water-borne minerals such as calcite, silica, or iron fill the open spaces that once held soft tissue. The hard portions of wood or bone are left alone. Sometimes, the hard parts decay and are replaced by minerals. This is known as **replacement**. Cell by cell, the minerals replace the hard parts to create an exact duplicate of the original. Australian miners tunneling through sandstone for gem opals sometimes stumble on shellfish and dinosaur bones fossilized in opal. Opal is a mineral made up of silicon, oxygen, and water. One of the most famous finds is "Eric," the partial skeleton of an opalized pliosaur. Pliosaurs are a type of marine reptile that lived 200 million years ago. Fossils leave their impressions behind for petrification. If an entire life form decays, it may leave a hollow cavity, or **mold**, in the sediment. A mold that becomes filled with minerals is called a **cast**. Trace fossils are molds and casts.

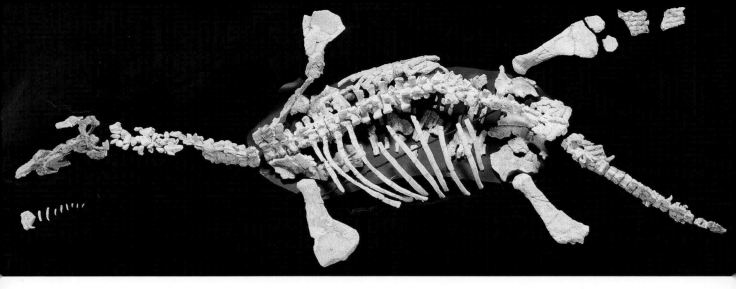

Plants, invertebrates, and fish are preserved through a process called carbonization. The pressure of sedimentary layers squeezes out all the liquids and gases inside the organism. This leaves an impression, along with a thin film of black or brown carbon, on the forming rock. Sometimes the carbon film is washed away, leaving only the imprint behind. The Burgess Shale, located in the Canadian Rockies, contains numerous carbonized fossils of soft-bodied marine creatures. The details of these 500-million-year-old organisms are so well-preserved that more than 140 types of extinct animal have been discovered there.

Eric's partial skeleton is on display as part of the National Opal Collection in Sydney, Australia.

Painted Desert

Arizona's 90,000-acre (36,500-hectare) Petrified National Park is home to the world's largest petrified "forest." Two hundred million years ago, fallen coniferous trees were buried by sediments rich in silica and other minerals that gradually replaced the wood. Traces of iron, manganese, and carbon painted the petrified logs in a vibrant palette of oranges, reds, and yellows.

Fossils like this carnivorous worm have been found in the Burgess Shale.

Freezing seems to stop time in its tracks as it entombs animals in ice. Entire rhinoceroses, bison, mammoths, mastodons, and even humans have been found fossilized in ice. The freezing process preserves internal organs, stomach contents, and even fur. Because minerals do not replace the original organic matter and no rock imprint is made, these specimens are often called sub-fossils. Most frozen fossils are found in arctic regions, mainly Alaska and Siberia, Russia. They date back to the end of the last ice age, about ten thousand years ago.

Another way fossils may be preserved is in organic matter such as amber. Insects, spiders, and other small animals sometimes get caught in the sticky sap that oozes from pine and fir trees. The sap then hardens, trapping the organisms inside.

Over time, the life forms dry up and decay, leaving carbonized molds inside the amber.

Scientists have been able to extract small bits of **DNA** from insects sealed in amber. DNA, or deoxyribonucleic acid, is the genetic blueprint for cells in living things. None of this extracted DNA has ever been successfully **replicated**. Unlike in the movie *Jurassic Park*, there is little chance that DNA from insects fossilized in amber can be used to create new life. The extracted DNA has, however, allowed scientists to study how species have changed through time. Also, since blood-sucking insects are major carriers of disease, the DNA of ancient bloodsuckers might offer clues leading to new vaccines for viruses such as typhus, encephalitis, and Lyme disease.

Ancient Amber

In 1993, scientists obtained DNA from a 125-million-year-old weevil embedded in amber. This is the oldest DNA ever extracted from a fossil.

Forever preserved in amber, this fly is believed to be more than 30 million years old.

Petrified logs in a ravine near Blue Mesa in the Petrified Forest National Park, Arizona

Chapter Three

Digging Into the Past

For thousands of years, fossils have both captivated and baffled the people who uncovered them. People from some ancient cultures wore fossils as amulets that were thought to have magical or medicinal powers. Native Americans believed that the petrified trees in Arizona were weapons left behind from battles fought between the gods. By the seventeenth century, naturalists began to realize that fossils were the remains of earlier life forms. This brought up many questions. When did these life forms exist? Were they all extinct? And what could fossils reveal about the history of Earth?

In the mid-1600s, Danish scientist Nicholas Steno was one of the first to study the layers, or **strata**, of sedimentary rock. Steno noted that older sediments settled in the lower strata, while more recent ones rested in upper beds. This meant that fossils found in the top layer were younger than those found near the bottom. In the late 1700s, English civil engineer William Smith concluded that rocks containing the same fossils must be about the same age. Because they only lived at certain times in the past, **index fossils**, such as clams, snails, trilobites, and graptolites, could be used to help date particular rock strata. Scottish **geologist** James Hutton further contended that fossils proved that Earth was far older than a few thousand years, which was the estimate of Earth's age in the late 1700s. By comparing fossils from varying strata, scientists could also see how organisms **evolved**, or gradually changed,

Evolving Earth

Fossils, stratigraphy (the study of strata), and other geological discoveries revealed that 250 million years ago all of the continents joined for a short time to form a supercontinent called Pangaea. Gradually, Pangaea split apart, becoming the seven continents we know today. Continental drift is still at work, changing and shaping our world. Thanks to the satellites of the global positioning system (GPS) that orbit Earth and snap photographs from space, scientists have calculated that the continents are moving at an average rate of about 3 inches (8 cm) per year.

over time. They could, at last, begin to piece together a portrait of Earth's continents, climates, and catastrophes.

These discoveries led to the creation of a calendar called the **geologic time scale**. Complex organisms have existed within a very small period of Earth's 4.6-billion-year history. This 550-million-year time frame is known as the Phanerozoic Eon, meaning "time of life." The Phanerozoic Eon is divided into three eras—Paleozoic, or "ancient life"; Mesozoic, meaning "middle life"; and Cenozoic, or "new life." The eras are broken down into shorter periods. The blocks of time within the scale are changed and updated as scientists gather new information.

Two scales are used to help establish the time periods within the geologic time scale—the relative scale and the radiometric scale. The relative scale dates fossils by looking at different rock strata and comparing the evolutionary stages of the fossils in them. This estimate is called **relative age**. For example, if a dinosaur bone is identified as being from the Jurassic Period, then the relative age of the fossil is between 145 million and 213 million years old.

In the early twentieth century, the discovery of radioactivity gave scientists

Scottish geologist James Hutton inspects a tree.

Geologic Time Scale

Phanerozoic Eon

Era	Period	Time in MYA (Millions of Years Ago)	Life on Earth
Cenozoic	Quaternary	0*–2	Humans Mass extinction of large land mammals such as saber-toothed cats, mastodons, and mammoths
	Tertiary	2–65	Primates, large land mammals, birds, horses, camels, whales, dolphins, grasses
Mesozoic	Cretaceous	65*–145	Snakes, flowering plants Mass extinction of all dinosaurs, flying reptiles, and many marine life forms (all ammonites go extinct)
	Jurassic	145–213	Large dinosaurs, crocodiles, flying and marine reptiles, early birds
	Triassic	213*–248	Lizards, dinosaurs, turtles Mass extinction of many ammonites, brachiopods, amphibians, and reptiles
Paleozoic	Permian	248*–286	Early reptiles Worst mass extinction ever; included forest plants, reptiles, and many marine life forms such as trilobites, corals, and crinoids
	Pennsylvanian	286–325	Amphibians, flying insects, coniferous swamp forests
	Mississippian	325–360	Seed ferns

	Devonian	360*–410	Cartilaginous and bony fish, amphibians, ammonites, seed plants
	Silurian	410–440	Jawed fish, insects, land plants
	Ordovician	440*–505	Jawless fish, bivalves, freshwater plants
	Cambrian	505*–544	Marine invertebrates: sponges, trilobites, brachiopods, echinoderms, cnidarians
Precambrian Time		544–4,500	Worms, stromatolites, bacteria

* Mass extinctions occurred during these times, usually at the close of the period

the ability to calculate the numeric age, or **radiometric age**, of rocks. Radioactive elements such as potassium, thorium, and uranium are found naturally in the minerals that form rocks. Over long periods of time, these radioactive elements decay into other elements at a steady rate—potassium turns to argon, and thorium and uranium turn to lead. Scientists know exactly how long it takes for each "parent" element to decay into its "daughter" element. For example, by comparing the amount of argon in a rock to the amount of potassium that remains, scientists are able to calculate the rock's numeric age. Radiometric dating can only be used on certain types of rock. It cannot be used in sedimentary rock, in which fossils are found. Scientists test crystalline rocks found alongside sedimentary rock to determine the radiometric age of a fossil.

Lost in Time

Many times throughout Earth's history **mass extinctions** have wiped out entire animal and plant populations. An estimated 30 to 60 percent of the organism families that live during any one period die during a mass extinction. Extinctions can be triggered by many factors, such as the impact of an asteroid, continental drift, a drop in sea levels, or changes in climate. Some extinctions happened within a few hundred years. Others took millions of years to occur. Paleontologists use mass extinctions to mark the boundaries between periods. Sudden changes in the fossils found in rock strata indicate when these catastrophic events occurred.

Sixty-five million years ago, at the close of the Cretaceous Period, nearly half of the animal and plant families on Earth vanished, including all dinosaurs, large marine reptiles, and ammonites. A shift in climate began the extinction, which was hurried along by the impact of a 6-mile- (10-km-) wide asteroid that smashed into Mexico. The aftermath of this

Taking Our Toll

Did you know that we are in the middle of a mass extinction right now? Around the world, animals are going extinct at 20,000 species per year, more than one hundred times nature's usual rate. Humans are the main cause of this mass extinction. Introducing new species into areas and wiping out native species, hunting, pollution, and destroying habitat through logging, and farming are some of the reasons why more animals have disappeared in the last ten thousand years than at any other time in our planet's history.

huge asteroid crash likely caused enormous sea waves, huge dust clouds that entered the atmosphere, and massive habitat destruction around the globe.

The largest mass extinction of all time occurred at the end of the Permian Period. During that time, as many as 95 percent of all organisms were lost. Scientists have suggested many reasons for the event, from lowered sea levels to volcanic eruptions to an asteroid strike. Still, no one is certain what happened 250 million years ago to cause such world-wide devastation.

This painting by Donald E. Davis shows what it may have looked like when an asteroid slammed into what is now Mexico.

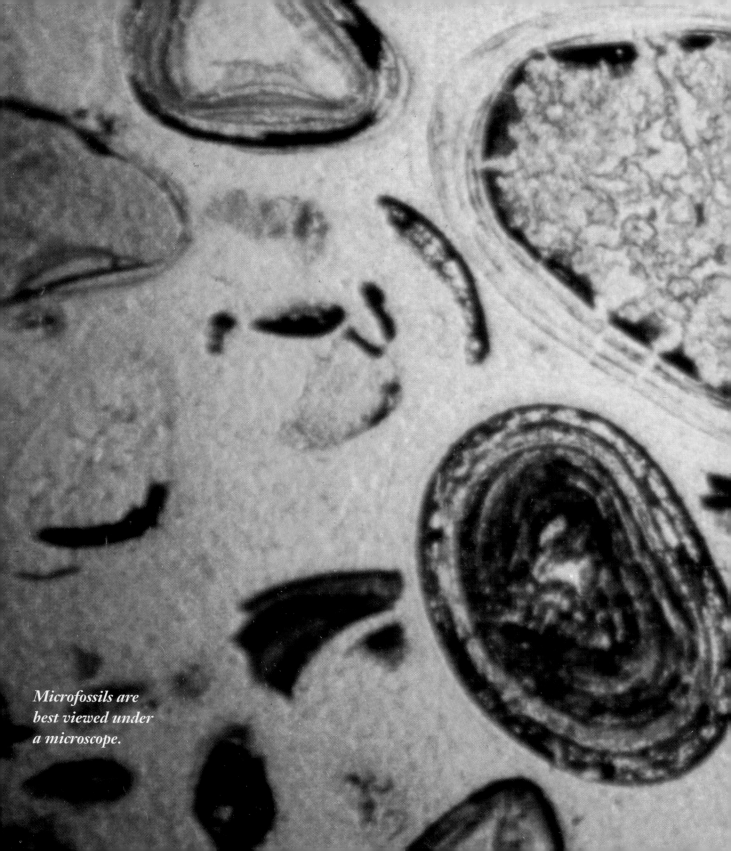

Microfossils are best viewed under a microscope.

Chapter Four

Fascinating Fossils

Whether it is an amber insect found on the Baltic coast or an Australian tree petrified in pearly opal, fossils open the door to a world that is long gone. To organize and study fossils, paleontologists place them into four main groups: plants, **microfossils**, **invertebrates**, and **vertebrates**. Microfossils are fossils that are so small, a microscope is needed to view them. Microfossils are tiny organisms such as algae, bacteria, pollen grains, seeds, and insect parts. Invertebrates are

Major Invertebrate Groups

Group	Examples
Sponges	tube sponges, glass sponges
Arthropods	insects, spiders, lobsters, crabs
Mollusks	snails, oysters, octopuses, clams
Echinoderms	sea cucumbers, sea urchins, sand dollars, starfish
Cnidarians	sea jellies, sea anemones, corals
Brachiopods	lamp shells

Fossils formed by cyanobacteria, called stromatolites, are among the oldest fossils to be found.

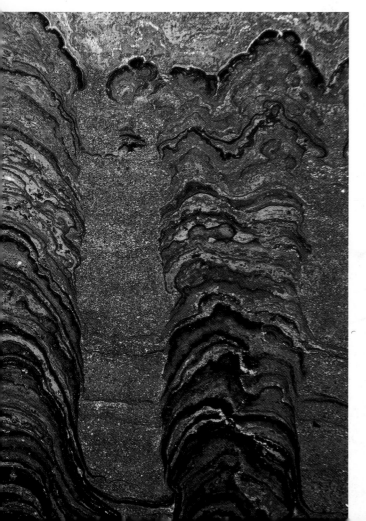

animals without backbones. Vertebrates are animals with backbones.

In this chapter, we will explore some of Earth's earliest life forms. Many of these plants and animals are extinct. The descendants of others live on, surviving and adapting to our ever-changing planet.

A Green World

The first tiny land plants appeared during the Silurian Period, more than 400 million years ago. At this time there was plenty of carbon dioxide and sunshine available for photosynthesis. Early plants adapted to life out of the

The oldest fossils on record are 3.5-billion-year-old mounds called **stromatolites**. These trace fossils are formed by cyanobacteria. Cyanobacteria use the light of the Sun to convert carbon dioxide and water into energy, releasing oxygen into the air as a waste product. Long ago, this process, called **photosynthesis**, helped to create an atmosphere that could support animal life on Earth. Cyanobacteria are far from extinct. You can still find these single-celled organisms growing in the warm, shallow waters of Shark Bay, Australia.

water and evolved strong stems. Plants such as *Rhynia*, a 6-inch (15-cm) reedlike plant, and *Cooksonia*, a branching sprig with round spores, had tough stalks but no leaves or flowers.

During the Pennsylvanian Period, Earth's climate was generally warm and damp. Primitive ginkgoes and conifers, which are cone-bearing fir and pine trees, appeared. Thick forest of ferns, horsetails, and club mosses sprouted in the tropical environment. Some grew like trees, reaching heights of 100 feet (30 m) or more. Unlike modern trees, they had short lives and were not woody. Some even had hollow trunks. One type of club moss, called *Lepidodendron*, grew to 130 feet (40 m) in length. Its fossil is distinguished by a spiral diamond pattern of scales on its bark. These were leaf bases—scars left behind when stems grew and the grasslike leaves fell off. Leafy plants became food for the first land vertebrates.

Found in a rock in Scotland, this fossil shows the stem of a Rhynia *plant.*

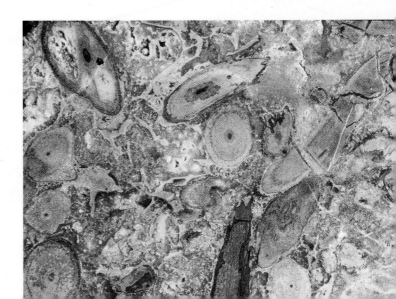

This is a fossil sample of Lepidodendron, *a type of club moss.*

Perishing Plants

Scientists estimate that 90 percent of the plant species that have ever lived on Earth are now extinct.

Tiny spiders, mites, and scorpions lived in the leaf litter that carpeted the ground. Today, we look to the fossil remains of these ancient swamp forests to provide much of the coal that fuels our world.

Angiosperms, or flowering plants, developed toward the end of the Cretaceous Period. This group includes flowering trees, cacti, shrubs, flowers, and grasses. Angiosperms are the most abundant plants on Earth today. There are more than 250,000 different species.

Plants are among the most extraordinary and beautiful fossils. The impression left behind by an oak or maple leaf may be so well preserved that each delicate vein is clearly visible in stone. It is extremely rare to find a fossil of an actual flower or bud—most are simply too fragile and wither too quickly to fossilize. Likewise, tropical plants do not fossilize well because they are broken down rapidly by bacteria in the soil.

It can sometimes be challenging for a **paleobotanist**, a scientist who studies plant fossils, to identify a particular fossil. Many different types of ancient plants had leaves, stems, and roots that were quite similar to one another. The task is made even more difficult because whole plants rarely fossilized. Often, identification must be made from a fossil of only a tiny part of the plant. Amateur fossil hunters are often fooled by "fake ferns." When this happens, what appears to be a

Each vein of the maple leaf is clearly visible in this fossil.

fossilized fern is really manganese oxide, a mineral deposit that grows in a dendritic, or fernlike, pattern on stone.

Intriguing Invertebrates

More than 500 million years ago, invertebrate life was plentiful in Earth's seas. **Sponges**, simple animals without nerves, muscles or glands, attached themselves to rocks or to the ocean floor. Their spiny skeletons, made of minerals such as calcite or silica, could be as small as 1 inch (2.5 cm) or larger than 2 feet (60 cm). Sponges have changed very little over time, although today's varieties are generally larger and more branchlike.

Cnidarians, such as corals, sea jellies, and sea anemones were also common in ancient oceans. Linked together, **colonies** of coral stretched to form reefs several miles long in tropical waters. Corals, like their cnidarian relatives, sting and kill prey with the tentacles ringing their mouths. Two groups of corals—rugose and tubulate—are extinct, but their fossils

are some of the most abundant on Earth. Modern types of corals flourish today, just as their ancestors did long ago.

Brachiopods, or lamp shells, are animals enclosed in two ridged shells connected by a hinge. Brachiopods filter food from the water using feeding tentacles. Most brachiopods have a thin, fleshy stalk called a pedicle that sticks out of the shell and anchors the animal to the sea floor or to other shells. Brachiopods are often confused with **bivalves**, such as oysters, clams, and mussels, but the shells of the two animals are different. While bivalves thrive today, brachiopod populations decreased significantly during a mass extinction 250 million years ago. Of the 3,500 known types of brachiopods that once lived on Earth, fewer than one hundred

Coral fossils are found all over the world. This Colonial Horn Coral fossil was found in Kentucky.

Brachiopods were very common in Paleozoic and Mesozoic times, but only a few species survive today.

Lilies of the Sea

Crinoids, which are echinoderms related to starfish and sand dollars, earned the nickname "sea lilies" because of their long stems, flowering arms, and cup-shaped body. These animals use their flowing arms to push food from the water toward their mouth. Most of today's crinoids, often called feather stars, do not have stems. Shallow-water crinoids may be bright red or yellow in color, while some are even striped.

remain. In the Pacific Ocean, they can be found in cold waters around Japan, Australia, Chile, and the Pacific Northwest Coast of the United States and Canada. Brachiopods are also abundant along the North Atlantic coastline.

This fossil of a moss animal is from the Mississippian Period.

Give Me a *G*

Graptolites, which were tiny sea organisms, built colonies of linking cups that floated with the ocean currents. Graptolite means "writing on rock," which is what these fossils are often mistaken for. Colonies sometimes formed letters of the alphabet, mainly O, Q, X, and Y, on rock. Graptolites went extinct 300 million years ago.

Bryozoans, also called moss animals, are tiny organisms that live in colonies and filter food from the water. They build networks of tiny tubes that resemble upright, wavy fans or flat, sheetlike mats. Fossilized bryozoan colonies have been found measuring up to 2 feet (60 cm) in length, but living bryozoans can be much harder to find. Although there are more than 3,500 types of living bryozoans, an entire colony might be less than 1 inch (2.5 cm) in length.

In Cambrian times, **nautiloids** were among the ocean's main predators. These **mollusks** were part of the cephalopod family and related to octopuses, squids, and cuttlefish. Early nautiloids lived in straight shells, while some later types had coiled ones. They varied in size from 1 inch (2.5 cm) to 13 feet (4 m) across. Only one type of nautiloid exists today—the nautilus. **Ammonites**, relatives of nautiloids, appeared in the Paleozoic Era. They made their homes in a variety of shell shapes, from Us to spires to irregular twists, some as large as 8 feet (2 m) wide. Scientists think that the chambered shells could be emptied or filled with water and gas to control buoyancy. Since ammonite shells were so thin, most fossils are internal molds made of calcite. Some others

Bit of a Trilobite

Many trilobite fossils did not form from actual animals, but from their fossilized exoskeletons, which the animals had to shed periodically to grow.

were formed by iron pyrites, often called "fool's gold." Ammonites went extinct 65 million years ago.

On the floors of prehistoric seas, more than ten thousand species of **trilobites** flourished. These **arthropods**, early relatives of crabs and lobsters, could be tinier than 1 inch (2.5 cm) or larger than 3 feet (1 m) in length. Trilobite means "three lobes." The name refers to the three body sections of the animal. Trilobites had a hard outer covering, or **exoskeleton**. Hinges allowed some types of trilobite to roll up into armored balls for protection, while others had long spikes that kept enemies at bay. Trilobites were among the first sea creatures to have complex eyes. It appears that most species had good eyesight, although some were blind. Trilobites went extinct 250 million years ago.

Cretaceous ammonites are mollusks with mother-of-pearl shells that can still glow after 65 million years.

Found in the Wolcho River in Russia, these are both trilobite fossils.

A Fish Story: Early Vertebrates

Fishes were the world's earliest vertebrates, first appearing on Earth about 530 million years ago. The oldest fishes, called **agnathans**, had a mouth but no jaws. Early fossils show that

You can clearly see the bony armor plating that protected this jawed fish.

agnathans had tough head shields, eyes on top of their head, and a mouth on the underside of their body that could suck food from the seafloor. Living lampreys and hagfish may be the descendants of these primitive fishes, although they do not have armored head shields. Hagfish usually feed on dead fishes, while lampreys are parasites. They latch onto larger fishes to suck out blood.

Agnathans were soon joined by a variety of fishes with jaws and bony armor plating. Although they had no teeth, they did have sharp, bony points and ridges at the edges of their jaws to capture and kill prey. At more than 30 feet (9 m) in length, *Dunkleosteus* was one of the largest jawed fishes. It had a shielded head and jaws enormous enough to have swallowed anything that lived in the ocean at that time.

Sharks, rays, and skates appeared during the Silurian Period. These fishes have skeletons made of **cartilage** rather than bone. Cartilage is a tough, rubbery tissue that supports the bones in the human ears, nose, and joints. Cartilage does not fossilize well, so fossils of shark skeletons are very rare. But shark teeth, which are made of tough calcium, are abundant. Paleontologists often rely on partial skeletons and teeth to

What a Catch!

In 1938, a fishing trawler netted an unusual fish off the coast of Africa. The fish had gills, lungs, and thick, muscular lobes where the fins attached to the body. When professor J.L.B. Smith identified it as a coelacanth (SEE-luh-canth)—a fish thought to be long extinct—the discovery made headlines. Since then, many more of these "living fossils" have been found in the waters near Madagascar and Indonesia. In 1998, a coelacanth population was found off the Indonesian island of Sulawesi.

Look at the size of the Carcharocles megalodon *tooth (right) compared to a tooth of a Great White shark.*

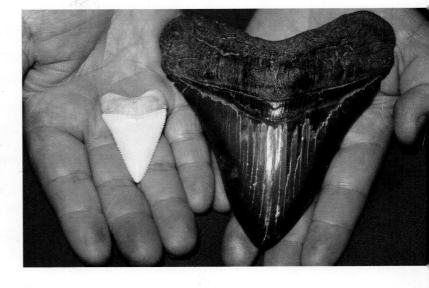

figure out what an ancient shark might have looked like. The discovery of a 7-inch (11-cm) tooth of the extinct shark *Carcharocles megalodon* helped paleontologists calculate that these enormous creatures measured up to 50 feet (15 m) in length and weighed more than 100,000 pounds (45,000 kilograms).

This is a frontal view of the fossilized remains of a gogo fish. Now extinct, gogo fish were a type of fish known as placoderms.

Chapter Five

The Search for Dinosaurs and Mammals

It's a blistering July afternoon in Hell Creek, Montana. But a team of paleontologists cannot afford to rest. They have discovered a partial *Tyrannosaurus rex*, or *T. rex*, skeleton sticking out of a cliff. *T. rex* was one of the largest **theropods**, or meat-eating, and scavenging dinosaurs that ever lived on Earth. It measured more than 40 feet (12 m) in length. Sixty

In this colored engraving from 1883, people are viewing an Iguanadon *dinosaur.*

ridged teeth, each up to 7 inches (18 cm) in length, lined its powerful jaws.

Although much of the dinosaur fossil is buried deep in rock, the crew must use hand tools to reach it, or else they could damage the bones. Day after day, hour after hour, they painstakingly chip away at the sandstone with picks and shovels. As more of the fossil is exposed, the tools must be traded for brushes that will gently remove dirt. Some rock is left around the bone to protect it. It will be removed carefully in the laboratory later on. Once the dinosaur skeleton is revealed, the bones will be numbered, photographed, and mapped. This is done so the skeleton can be pieced together correctly later on. A deep trench is dug around the dinosaur. Strips of fabric are dipped in plaster and layered onto the bones. Just as a cast keeps a broken leg in place, the hardened plaster will protect the fossils while they are being moved to a laboratory.

What's In a Name?

In 1676, Robert Plot, a professor at Oxford University, was the first to write about dinosaurs—but he didn't realize it at the time. He thought the large bone he had seen was from an enormous ancient human. It was actually the thigh bone of a meat-eating *Megalosaurus.* After studying fossils of *Megalosaurus* and the plant-eating *Iguanadon,* British paleontologist Sir Richard Owen coined the term "dinosaur." It means "terrible lizard."

The Real Jurassic Park

Throughout the Mesozoic era and until their extinction 65 million years ago, dinosaurs ruled the land. No one can be sure just how many dinosaurs roamed prehistoric Earth, but more than 850 types of dinosaur fossils have been discovered on every continent, even Antarctica. Nowhere on the planet are dinosaur bones more abundant than in North America. Dinosaur National Monument is one of the largest dinosaur graveyards. It stretches across more than 200,000 acres in northeastern Utah and northwestern Colorado. Bones of more than half of all the different types of dinosaurs that lived in North America during the late Jurassic Period have been discovered at the quarry.

Uncovered by American paleontologist Earl Douglass in 1909, Dinosaur National Monument has yielded hundreds of tons of fossil bones of theropods, such as *Ceratosaurus*, *Allosaurus*, and *Stegosaurus*. *Stegosaurus* is noted for the series of large triangular plates attached to its spine. The plates may have been used for protection, to attract a mate, and to regulate body temperature by absorbing or giving off heat.

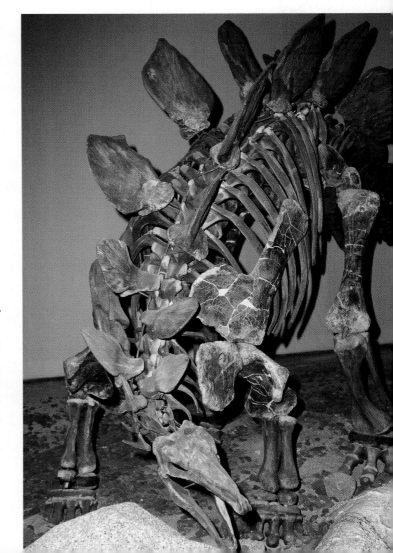

In this picture you can clearly see the plates attached to the spine of this Stegosaurus *fossil.*

Putting the Pieces Together

Try reconstructing an animal you've never seen before, especially when its bones have been scattered throughout a fossil site, jumbled, or lost altogether. In the 1820s, fossils of *Iguanodon* were among the first dinosaur bones ever found. The only clues scientists had to piece together the 30-foot (9-m) beast were a few bones, some teeth, and a horn. It wasn't until fifty years later, when a number of complete *Iguanodon* skeletons were found in a Belgian coal mine, that scientists realized they had made a serious mistake. The horn they had stuck on the top of the dinosaur's snout was really a spike that belonged on its thumb.

The quarry is also home to the fossils of huge, thin-necked, plant-eating sauropods, including *Barosaurus*, *Diplodocus*, and *Apatosaurus*. Sauropods were the largest dinosaurs on Earth. They could weigh more than 90 tons and reach lengths of 130 feet (40 m). Most sauropods walked on four thick legs, swinging their long tails behind them. The tail of *Apatosaurus* was almost one and a half times the length of its 80-foot (24-m) body.

Trapped in Time

Every day, more than 8 gallons (32 liters) of hot, sticky oil bubbles to the surface at the Rancho La Brea Tar Pits. The tar pits are located in the heart of Los Angeles, California. Once in a while, the asphalt catches the foot of an unsuspecting tourist in its gooey grip in the same way it has been trapping animals since the last ice age. Between 10,000 and 40,000 years ago, bison, horses, wolves, camels, saber-toothed cats,

When Time Stopped

At Ashfall Fossil Beds in Nebraska, whole herds of rhinoceroses, camels, horses, and elephants appear to be frozen in an instant. Ten million years ago, a volcanic blast from the Rocky Mountains sent clouds of hot ash across Nebraska. Hundreds of animals were buried alive in ash up to 8 feet (2 m) deep. The animals were so well-preserved that some had fossilized grass in their mouths.

mammoths, and mastodons came to drink the water that pooled on top of the tar. Some of these animals found themselves stuck in the gluey asphalt. When a large creature got caught, it would attract predators who would then find themselves snagged too. This attracted still more predators. Since the early 1900s, scientists have uncovered more than three million plant and animal fossils within the pits. Although most fossils are altered from their original forms in some way, the bones recovered at La Brea are still well-preserved.

Below left: *Excavation volunteers dig in a pit at the La Brea Tar Pits.*

Below right: *This bone, sticking out of the tar at the La Brea Tar Pits, is a thigh bone of a saber-toothed tiger.*

La Brea Woman

In 1914, the partial skeleton of a female was unearthed at La Brea. Scientists estimate that the woman lived more than 9,000 years ago and suffered a serious skull injury. How and why she ended up in the pits remains a mystery.

During the Cenozoic Era, which followed the extinction of the dinosaurs, **mammals** diversified and became larger. Rhinoceroses, saber-toothed cats, horses, ground sloths, and camels standing 10 feet (3 m) high roamed the continents. Mastodons and mammoths were among the biggest mammals ever to live on land. Mastodons had muscular trunks and large heads and bodies. Ranging from 8 to 10 feet (2 to 3 m) in height and weighing more than 8,000 pounds (3,700 kg), mastodons were slightly smaller than their mammoth cousins. Mammoths had tusks that grew to 10 feet (3 m) in length, long trunks, shaggy fur, and humps on their backs. The largest mammoth fossil ever discovered measured 14 feet (4 m) high at the shoulder. Fossil skeletons of mammoths and mastodons have been found in the frozen ground in arctic regions such as Alaska and northern Asia.

Between 9,000 and 12,000 years ago, many of the larger land mammals, including mammoths and mastodons, went extinct. Scientists debate about why these creatures died out. Some believe early humans hunted them to extinction, while other says it's possible that germs and diseases introduced by humans wiped out these giants of the land.

It is these kinds of baffling mysteries that keep paleontologists in the field, digging for answers. From the tiniest single-celled organisms to giant mammoths, fossils are our link to what life was like on our planet before the dawn of humans. Each new fossil discovery is a piece of the past, a clue to our history long buried by the sands of time.

Models of mammoths are on display at the La Brea Tar Pits.

Students comb a hillside for fossils.

Chapter Six

Treasure Hunters

Fossils are nature's gifts to us. Their beauty and history make them extraordinary treasures. Paleontologists are not the only ones who have found fossils long buried by the sands of time. Amateur collectors have made important fossil discoveries. As a young girl, Mary Anning scoured the beach for shells to sell at her father's seaside souvenir shop in England. In 1811, when she was just 12 years old, Anning uncovered the first complete skeleton of an *Ichthyosaur*, a

There may be places near where you live that hold fossil remains.

a dolphinlike reptile with a pointed snout and flippers that lived 200 million years ago. Over her lifetime, Anning made many more contributions to the world of paleontology. She is perhaps best remembered for the tongue twister she inspired: "She sells seashells by the seashore."

If you are interested in fossil hunting, you should explore river and creek beds, ocean shorelines, quarries, gravel pits, and road cuts—places where a roadway has been cut through rock. Before you begin your search, here are a few safety tips to keep in mind.

- When hunting for fossils, always take an adult with you.
- Wear appropriate clothing, boots, and gloves (to protect your hands).
- Take food, water, and a first-aid kit if you are planning to be outdoors longer than a few hours.
- Don't trespass on private property, federal land, or construction sites.
- Don't take rocks that cannot be lifted out of the ground easily.
- Stay away from cliffs, overhangs, deep canyons, and swift rivers.

For more safety tips, help in locating fossil sites, and a guide to identifying fossil discoveries, check your local library for guidebooks. Visit local universities and museums to see fossils on display and to learn more about their amazing histories. You can also log on to the U.S. Geological Survey's Web site at *http://www.usgs.gov* for information on fossils, the geologic time scale, and careers in paleontology.

A Rare Find

In 1982, amateur fossil hunter Bill Walker discovered a large claw in a muddy quarry in Surrey, England. Paleontologists dug up the partial skeleton and, to their surprise, realized they had unearthed a new species of dinosaur. They named their find *Baryonyx walkeri* in honor of Walker.

Glossary

agnathans—primitive fish that did not have jaws

amber—fossilized tree resin, or sap

ammonites—an extinct group of mollusks; squidlike animals that lived in coiled, spiraled, or U-shaped shells

angiosperm—a class of flowering plants

arthropods—a group of invertebrates that have exoskeletons and jointed legs

badlands—an eroded landscape in a dry region where there is little vegetation, and rainwater drains quickly

bivalves—invertebrate marine and freshwater mollusks characterized by two shells connected by a single hinge

brachiopods—invertebrate marine animals with two hinged shells enclosing a primitive filter-feeding body

bryozan—tiny organism that lives in colonies and filters food from the water

carbonization—a process of fossilization by which a residue or film of carbon is formed

cartilage—the tough, rubbery tissue that makes up the skeletons of sharks, rays, and other fish

cast—a type of fossil in which the skeletal parts of the organism have been dissolved and the resulting space replaced by other materials, usually minerals

climate—the prevailing weather conditions of a particular area, averaged over more than thirty years

cnidarians—simple marine invertebrates characterized by tentacles

colony—a group of genetically related individuals that may be linked together to form an organism

coprolites—fossilized pieces of animal dung

DNA (deoxyribonucleic acid)—the genetic blueprint of cells

dinosaur—a member of a group of extinct reptiles that appeared during the Triassic Period and became extinct at the end of the Cretaceous Period

echinoderms—invertebrate marine animals characterized by a body divided into five parts, a skeleton of interconnecting plates, and a brittle, spiny outer covering

erode—to wear away or transport an object by forces such as wind, water, ice, and gravity

evolve—to change over time

extinct—no longer existing

exoskeleton—a hard, external covering secreted by animals such as trilobites and lobsters

fossil—preserved evidence that an organism once lived on Earth; preserved organisms are **body fossils**, while **trace fossils** are the marks animals leave behind, such as footprints, tail tracks, nests, eggs, and dung

fossil fuels—naturally occurring fuels, such as coal, oil, and natural gas, formed slowly underground by the action of heat on the remains of dead plants and animals

freezing—a process of fossilization whereby an animal or plant is preserved in ice

geologist—a scientist who studies the origin, structure, and composition of Earth

geologic time scale—a chronological series of events in the geological history of Earth determined by fossil discoveries

graptolites—tiny sea organisms that built colonies of linking cups that floated with ocean currents

index fossils—fossils that appear in certain rock strata during certain time periods

invertebrates—animals without backbones

mammal—a warm-blooded, or endothermic, vertebrate characterized by hair or fur, a highly developed brain, and the ability to nurse its young

mass extinction—the widespread death of plant and animals species in which more than 30 percent of existing families are wiped out during a particular time period

microfossil—a fossil so small that a microscope is needed to study it

mollusks—a group of invertebrate animals that usually secrete a hard shell

mold—a fossil in which the original skeletal parts have dissolved away, leaving a space that preserves their shape; the filling of a mold is called a **cast**

nautiloids—invertebrate marine cephalopods that live in straight or coiled shells

paleobotanist—a scientist who studies Earth's plant fossils

paleontologist—a scientist who studies Earth's fossils

permineralization—a process of petrification whereby water-borne minerals fill the open spaces that once held soft tissue, while the hard portions are left alone

petrification—the partial or complete conversion of an organism into rock

photosynthesis—the process by which plants and other organisms use light from the Sun to convert carbon dioxide and water into food, releasing oxygen into the air as a waste product

prehistoric—occurring before humans' recorded events

radiometric age—the age of a rock calculated by measuring the ratio of decay of one radioactive element to another

relative age—the dating of rocks or fossils using only their relative sequences in rock strata

replacement—a process of petrification whereby minerals

replace the hard parts of an organism cell by cell, to create an exact duplicate of the original

replicate—to reproduce

sauropods—a group of herbivorous dinosaurs belonging to the order of saurischians that are characterized by large bodies, long necks, tiny heads, and elephantlike legs

sedimentary rock—a type of rock made up of sediment, such as clay, silt, or sand, that has been compacted and cemented together

sponge—a simple animal without nerves, muscles, or glands

strata—layers of sedimentary rock originally formed in horizontal beds in which the oldest rocks are at the bottom and the youngest are at the top

stromatolites—limestone mounds formed by cyanobacteria

theropods—the group of carnivorous, or meat-eating, dinosaurs

trilobite—an extinct arthropod group that lived on Earth from 540 to 250 million years ago

vertebrates—animals with backbones

To Find Out More

Books

Arnold, Caroline. *Giant Shark: Megalodon, Prehistoric Predator*. New York: Clarion Books, 2000.

Dingus, Lowell, and Luis Chiappe. *The Tiniest Giants: Discovering Dinosaur Eggs*. New York: Random House, 1999.

Kittinger, Jo. *Stories in Stone: The World of Animal Fossils*. New York: Grolier, 1998.

Lessem, Don. *Dinosaurs to Dodos: An Encyclopedia of Extinct Animals*. New York: Scholastic, 1999.

Relf, Pat. *A Dinosaur Named Sue: The Story of the Colossal Fossil*. New York: Scholastic, 2000.

Taylor, Paul. *Fossil*. New York: Dorling Kindersley, 2000.

Thompson, Sharon Elaine. *Deathtrap: The Story of the La Brea Tar Pits*. Minneapolis, MN: Lerner Publications, 1995.

Videos

Valley of the T-Rex. Discovery Channel Video, 2001.

Three Minutes to Impact. Discovery Channel Video, 2001.

CD-ROMs

Dinosaur Hunter. Dorling Kindersley, 1996.

Grolier's Prehistoria: The Multimedia Who's Who of Prehistoric Life. Grolier, 1994.

Earthquest. Dorling Kindersley, 1997.

Organizations and Online Sites

American Museum of Natural History
79th Street and Central Park West
New York, NY 10024
http://www.amnh.org
Take an online virtual tour of the museum to explore the fossils of extinct animals such as ammonites and dinosaurs, as well as "living fossils" like the coelacanth.

George C. Page Museum
La Brea Tar Pits
5801 Wilshire Blvd.
Los Angeles, CA 90036
http://www.tarpits.org
Discover what California was like at the close of the last Ice Age as you explore the oozing world of the tar pits and the 565 species of animal that have been trapped in time. Learn how paleontologists must excavate the site carefully. Read about some of the incredible fossils they have uncovered, including saber-toothed cats, camels, mastodons, and mammoths.

National Geographic Society
PO Box 98199
Washington, DC 20090-8199
http://www.nationalgeographic.com
http://www.nationalgeographic.com/dinoeggs
See what Earth was like when dinosaurs roamed the planet, learn about mass extinctions, and go along as paleontologists search for dinosaur nesting grounds. Log on to the Web site to see virtual-reality images of what scientists believe dinosaur embryos really looked like.

U.S. Geological Survey
509 National Center
Reston, Virginia 20192

http://www.usgs.gov
http://ask.usgs.gov

This government organization provides information regarding natural resources, natural disasters, and other geological data to the public. At the USGS Web site, you can dig into the past and discover just how scientists determine the ages of rocks and fossils. Learn more about radiometric dating, evolution, and get the most up-to-date version of the geologic time scale. If you have a question about fossils or paleontology, you can ask a geologist on-line.

A Note on Sources

Science continues to break new ground on fossil discoveries at a dizzying pace. In 2001, the first complete skull of *Sarcosuchus* (sar-koh-SOOK-us), the largest crocodile ever known to have lived on the planet, was unearthed in Africa. Paleontologists say the giant croc, which lived about 110 million years ago, measured up to 40 feet (12 m) in length, weighed 18,000 pounds (8,300 kg), and probably preyed on dinosaurs with its massive 4-foot (1-m) jaws. Yet another small piece of Earth's massive historical puzzle has been put into place.

I consulted many sources on the far-reaching topic of fossils, among them the U.S. Geological Survey, the American Museum of Natural History, the Paleontological Research Institution, the Museum of Paleontology at the University of California at Berkeley, the Peabody Museum of Natural History, and the National Museum of Natural History at the Smithsonian Institution in Washington, D.C.

Books such as *A Fish Caught in Time: The Search for the Coelacanth*, by Samantha Weinberg; *Trilobite! Eyewitness to Evolution*, by Richard Fortey; and *The Quest for Life in Amber*, by George and Roberta Poinar provided valuable in-depth and historical views of the subject. Books written for young readers, video documentaries, interactive CD-Rom titles, and firsthand observations at local museums helped round out my studies.

Finally, special thanks to Dr. Elizabeth Nesbitt, Curator of Invertebrate Paleontology at the Burke Museum of Natural History and Culture at the University of Washington. Her expertise, guidance, heartfelt enthusiasm, and strong commitment to educating children are evident in every page of this book.

—*Trudi Strain Trueit*

Index

Numbers in *italics* indicate illustrations.

About the Author

Trudi Strain Trueit is an award-winning television news reporter, weather forecaster, and freelance journalist. She has contributed stories to ABC News, CBS News, and CNN. Trueit has a B.A. in broadcast journalism. She has written many books for the Watts Library Earth Science series, including *Rocks, Gems, and Minerals*; *Earthquakes*; *Volcanoes*; *Clouds*; *Storm Chasers*; *The Water Cycle*; and *Rain, Hail, and Snow*.

Trueit's fascination with fossils began with childhood trips to the Washington coast. A beachcomber at heart, she still loves hunting for sand dollars and other fossil treasures on the stormy shores of the Pacific. Trueit makes her home in Everett, Washington, with her husband, Bill.

Juv
560
TRU

SEP 0 6 2003